Russell Thacher Trall

The Hygeian Home Cook-Book

Or, healthful and palatable food without condiments

Russell Thacher Trall

The Hygeian Home Cook-Book
Or, healthful and palatable food without condiments

ISBN/EAN: 9783744789202

Printed in Europe, USA, Canada, Australia, Japan

Cover: Foto ©Lupo / pixelio.de

More available books at **www.hansebooks.com**

THE
HYGEIAN HOME COOK-BOOK

OR, HEALTHFUL AND

PALATABLE FOOD WITHOUT CONDIMENTS.

BY

R. T. TRALL, M. D.

AUTHOR OF "HYDROPATHIC ENCYCLOPÆDIA;"
"HYDROPATHIC COOK-BOOK;" "HYGIENIC HAND BOOK;" "THE
TRUE HEALING ART;" "DIGESTION AND DYSPEPSIA;"
"THE BATH;" "WATER-CURE FOR THE MILLION;"
"THE MOTHER'S HYGIENIC HAND-BOOK," AND
VARIOUS OTHER WORKS.

———

NEW-YORK:
S. R. WELLS, PUBLISHER, 389 BROADWAY.
1874.

Entered according to Act of Congress, in the year 1874, by
SAMUEL R. WELLS,
In the office of the Librarian of Congress, at Washington, D. C.

BROOKLYN, N. Y.
STEREOTYPED BY THE ORPHANS ON THE CHURCH CHARITY FOUNDATION.

PREFACE

THE work now offered to the public is an explanation of our mode of cooking at "Hygeian Home." More than twenty years ago the "Hydropathic Cook Book" was published, as an exposition of the theory and practice of cookery adapted to that age and stage of the Dietetic Reformation; and that work is still commended to those who desire a more complete treatise on diet, with a plan for plain and wholesome cooking.

But for a dozen years past our table for invalids has been prepared without the employment of milk, sugar, salt, yeast, acids, alkalies, grease, or condiments of any kind. Our only seasonings have been fruits and other foods in a normal state, so prepared and combined as to produce the requisite flavor to please without perverting the taste.

As our institution stands alone among all the real or pretended health institutions in the world in this respect, we have taken much pains and made many experiments to improve every article and perfect every dish; and we have reason to believe that all persons who desire pure and palatable food, and who wish to "eat to live," will find ample directions in this little volume.

Among the special advantages of the plan we have adopted, so far as invalids are concerned, is the absence of sour stomach, biliousness, and constipation, so troublesome to all dyspeptics who use milk and sugar. Nor do our patients have any desire to drink at meals. Pure food never occasions thirst; and all physiologists know that taking water with food renders digestion and assimilation imperfect in all persons, and seriously interferes with the recovery of health by invalids.

As we use no seasonings, they are not mentioned in our recipes. But those who cannot change at once from high-seasoned to unseasoned food, may season to suit with anything they please, recollecting that the rule of health always is, the less the better. The recipes are good in their own merits; and it is for the reader to choose what concessions he will make to habit or vitiated appetences. He may be assured, however, that a little perseverance in the use of unseasoned food will generally soon restore the normal sensibilities, so that the purest food will be the most palatable.

FLORENCE HIGHTS, N. J.   R. T. T.

CONTENTS

PAGE

CHAPTER I—BREADS 9

General Rules—Premium Bread—Cold Water Loaf Bread—Hot Water Rolls—Hot Water Loaf Bread—Mush Rolls—Gems—Fruit Gems—Wheat-Meal Crisps—Oat-meal Crisps—Cocoanut Bread—Fruit Bread—Sweet Potato Bread—Sweet Potato Fruit Bread—White Potato Bread—Fancy Breads—Pumpkin Bread—Apple Bread—Snow Bread—Corn and Graham Bread—Farina and Graham Bread—Rye and Indian Bread—Mixed Meal Bread—Plain Johnny Cake—Pumpkin Johnny Cake—Rye Bread—Oat-meal Bread—Brown Bread—Berry Short Cake—Corn Dodgers—Rice Cakes—Berry Toast—Apple Toast—Rhubarb Toast—Whole Grains and Seeds.

CHAPTER II—MUSHES 21

General Rules—Crushed Wheat Mush—Corn Grits—Hominy—Farina—Oat-meal Mush—Corn-meal Mush—Graham Mush—Rye Mush—Berry Mush—Rice Mush.

CHAPTER III—PIES 25

General Rules—Graham Pie Crust—Mush Pie Crust—Oat-meal Pie Crust—Potato Pie Crust—Corn-meal Pie Crust—Cocoanut Pie Crust—Apple Pie—Berry Pie—Cranberry Pie—Rhubarb Pie—Pumpkin Pie—Stewed Apple Pie—Peach Pie—Pear Pie—Dried Fruit Pies—Cocoa-custard Pie—Tarts—Dumplings.

CHAPTER IV—PUDDINGS 31

General Rules—Hygienic Brown Betty—Indian Pudding—Corn Mush Pudding—Sweet Potato Pudding—Birds' Nest Pudding—Baked Apple Pudding—Sweet Apple Pudding—Rice and Apple Pudding—Snow Ball Pudding—Steamed Pudding.

CONTENTS.

CHAPTER V—SAUCES 35

General Rules—Cocoanut Sauce—Date Sauce—Lemon Sauce—Orange Sauce—Currant Sauce—Fig Sauce—Apple and Tomato Sauce—Dried Fruit Sauce—Grape and Apple Sauce—Shortcake Sauce.

CHAPTER VI—SOUPS 39

General Rules—Vegetable Soup—Tomato Soup—Split Pea Soup—Bean Soup—Green Bean Soup—Green Pea Soup—Spinach Soup—Vegetable and Rice Soup—Potato Soup—Asparagus Soup—Vegetable Broth—Barley Broth—Porridges—Gruels.

CHAPTER VII—VEGETABLES 44

General Rules — Model-cooked Potatoes — Boiled Potatoes — Boiled Peeled Potatoes—Mashed Potatoes—Browned Potatoes—Browned Mashed Potatoes—Baked Potatoes—Roasted Potatoes—Steamed Potatoes — Sweet Potatoes — Mashed Sweet Potatoes—Boiled Turnips—Browned Turnips—Boiled Beets—Chopped Beets and Tomatoes—Parsnips — Browned Parsnips — Carrots — Boiled Cabbage — Cabbage and Tomatoes — Cauliflower — Asparagus — Greens—Green Peas—Green Beans—Boiled Green Corn—Roasted Green Corn — Succotash — Garden Beans—Lima Beans — Boiled Dried Beans—Baked Dried Beans—Mashed Baked Beans—Beans and Cabbage—Split Peas—Dried Green Peas—Cucumbers.

CHAPTER VIII—FRUITS 55

General Rules—Baked Apples — Baked Apples with Dates—Baked Pared Apples—Steamed Apples—Stewed Apples—Stewed Dried Apples—Pears—Peaches—Stewed Dried Peaches—Apricots—Quinces—Pineapples—Cranberries—Blackberries—Whortleberries—Raspberries—Strawberries—Cherries—Plums—Currants — Gooseberries—Bananas — Oranges—Lemons—Tomatoes—Melons—Rhubarb—Pumpkin—Squash—Grapes — Prunes — English Dried Currants—Figs.

CHAPTER IX—PRESERVING FRUITS 64

General Rules—Berries—Strawberries—Grapes—Packing Grapes—Apples—Peaches—Pears— Tomatoes—Bananas — Rhubarb—Vegetables—Miss Jones' Invention.

CHAPTER I.

BREADS.

GENERAL RULES.

PERFECT bread is made of the meal of any kind of grain and pure water. It may be rendered as light, crisp, and tender as desirable by kneading or otherwise working atmospheric air into the dough. Water of any temperature may be employed in making the dough. Hot or boiling water renders the bread softer and damper, cool and cold water renders it more dry and brittle. But for the best possible article the water cannot be too cold. Iced-water renders the bread tender and most delicious, if the kneading is well managed.

Excellent bread may be made of wheat-meal, rye-meal, corn-meal, oat-meal, or of various admixtures of them, to please the fancy or suit the taste. Those who employ wheat-meal exclusively should see that the grain be plump, clean, and properly ground. In grinding it should be finely comminuted, or cut into small particles by sharp stones or hand mills. If ground with dull stones the branny portion will be rubbed off in flakes, and good light bread cannot be made of the article. The white wheat is more easily managed than the red, and makes a handsomer appearance on the table, although I cannot say that it is more wholesome than the red.

It is very important that the meal be freshly ground, as all meal or flour deteriorates continually. We have it fresh from the mill twice a week. Private families with hand mills can grind it fresh every day.

PREMIUM BREAD.

Mix unbolted wheat-meal (Graham flour) with pure cold water—the colder the better—to a stiff dough; knead thoroughly ten or fifteen minutes, or until the dough becomes elastic and spongy, and does not require the bread-board longer to be dusted with flour to prevent sticking as it is rolled out. For baking the dough may be rolled out and out into various forms, to suit taste or convenience. It may be made into rolls, squares, strips, rings, "diamonds," "fingers," etc., the object in all cases being to expose as much of the surface as possible to the heat of the oven.

The rolls and "fingers" are made three or four inches long and three-fourths of an inch thick; squares and diamonds are one to two inches in diameter (these require pricking), and one-half to three-fourths of an inch thick; strips may be three or four inches long, one inch wide, and one-fourth of an inch thick; rings are made by cutting out a circle of dough one-half to three-fourths of an inch in thickness, and three inches in diameter, then cutting out a ball from the centre of the circle one inch in diameter. The rings and balls present a beautiful appearance on the table, and no shape in which dough can be cut is in better condition for baking.

For baking, a quick oven is required. The bread should be placed immediately on the grates of the oven, never on tins; it should be placed in the hottest part of the oven at first, and removed back a little as soon as a crust is formed. Care must be taken to have the dough thoroughly baked, or it will become heavy when cold. The time required for baking is twenty to forty minutes, according to the size of the bread and the heat of the oven. When well done the bread has an elastic or spongy feeling.

COLD-WATER LOAF-BREAD.

This is mixed and kneaded in the same manner as the "Premium" bread; but is molded in a larger form, and baked in a more moderate heat, to insure its being thoroughly done in the centre, without burning the outside. It is usually made in loaves two-and-a-half to three-and-a-half inches thick, and of any length desired. It should be in the oven about one hour. If the crust is too hard, cover it in an earthen jar, or envelop it closely in a linen cloth until cold, when it is ready for the table. It should never be cut while hot.

HOT WATER ROLLS.

This is commonly called "soft bread." It is made by pouring boiling water over wheat-meal, and stirring with a strong spoon to a stiff dough; then kneaded quickly and rolled out into any desired form; "rolls" and "diamonds," are the best forms for this kind of bread. This bread has a very sweet flavor, and "new beginners" are very fond of it.

HOT WATER LOAF BREAD.

This is made in the same manner as the preceding, except that it is molded into long loaves, three or four inches thick. It requires baking about one hour in a moderate oven.

MUSH ROLLS.

These are made light, spongy, and soft enough for toothless persons, by mixing with cold mush of any kind, sufficient meal to form a soft dough; then rolled to the size of the thumb, and baked in a hot oven twenty or thirty minutes. A few English currants may be added to render them more palatable.

GEMS.

Stir into the coldest water any kind of meal and mix to a stiff batter, yet so that it may lift with a spoon and settle smooth of itself; drop immediately into hot gem pans (iron are best); let them stand on the top of the stove a few minutes, then bake in a hot oven thirty or forty minutes. When done they should be light and dry when broken. If mushy on the inside the batter was not thick enough. If the gem pans are hot and kept smooth no greasing is necessary.

FRUIT GEMS.

These are made in the same manner as the preceding, with the addition of any kind of dried fruit that may be preferred. Seedless currants, thoroughly washed and soaked in a very little water, or raisins stoned and stewed soft, are commonly preferred. The addition of a little grated cocoanut, makes an article of food which is simple, wholesome, and luxurious.

WHEAT-MEAL CRISPS.

Make a dough as for "Premium Bread;" roll to the thickness of a table knife blade; cut in any desired form; prick with a fork; put it on the grate in a hot oven, and watch closely to see that it becomes cooked and crisp without being browned. If well managed these crisps are delicious, very tender, and well adapted to those who have poor teeth.

OAT-MEAL CRISPS.

These may be made of oat-meal or oat-meal mush, mixed with boiling water to a stiff dough; then kneaded a little; mixed with a little wheat-meal to prevent its crumbling; moulded, cut into small thin cakes, and baked twenty or thirty minutes in a hot oven. If made very thin, and kept in a cool, dry place, they will retain a rich flavor for several days.

COCOANUT BREAD.

Add to three quarts of wheat-meal one grated cocoanut (or in that proportion); mix with water to a stiff dough; knead till the dough becomes spongy; mold into any desired form, and bake in a hot oven twenty to thirty minutes. This bread is a great favorite on festive occasions.

FRUIT BREAD.

Make a dough as for either of the first three kinds of bread; roll out the dough on the bread-board of any thickness desired; cover this with a mixture of the following fruits, or with either one or more of them: stoned raisins, stoned dates, English currants, and stewed figs; cocoanut may be grated over the fruit if its flavor is also desired; turn the dough over the fruit, and roll up tightly into a loaf, and bake in a hot oven. If made with cold water, as in "Premium" bread, it may be rolled in a cloth and steamed two or three hours. This is regarded as a very rich and savory dish, and also wholesome.

SWEET POTATO BREAD.

Boil sweet potatoes with the skins on, peal and mash through a colander; mix with an equal quantity of wheat-meal; if too moist add more wheat-meal; if too dry add a little boiling water; knead together quickly as for "Hot Water" bread, or roll it into "Diamonds," and bake in a quick oven.

SWEET POTATO FRUIT BREAD.

Make a dough as in the preceding recipe, adding grated cocoanut if desired; roll out thin and spread on any one or more kinds of fruit (raisins and figs are sufficient), mentioned in the recipe for "Fruit Bread;" make into a loaf and bake in a quick oven.

WHITE POTATO BREAD.

Wash and peel the potatoes; boil them in as little water as will cover them; mash them through a colander with the water in which they were boiled; heat the whole to the boiling point; mix in wheat-meal until sufficiently stiff to knead; cut into small cakes and bake in a hot oven. The flavor usually preferred is secured by using three parts of meal to one of potatoes.

FANCY BREADS.

Make "Sweet Potato Bread" as already mentioned; roll thin and cut into fanciful shapes with cake cutters, or make a dough as for "Premium Bread," adding freely of grated cocoanut, and roll thin and cut into any desirable forms; bake in a hot oven.

PUMPKIN BREAD.

Stew pumpkin very dry and mix with wheat-meal to a rather soft dough; make the dough into the shape of loaf bread, diamonds, rolls, or roll thin and divide into pieces with cake cutters.

APPLE BREAD.

This is made precisely as the preceding, substituting apple sauce for pumpkin. Sweet apples, and those of a mild acid flavor, are the best for this kind of bread.

SNOW BREAD.

Mix thoroughly together two parts of dry, clean snow, and one part of corn meal; turn the mass into an iron baking pan, and bake in a very hot oven. The bread should be one to one and a half inches in thickness.

CORN AND GRAHAM BREAD.

Take cold corn meal mush, and knead wheat-meal

into it till the mass becomes a soft dough ; shape it into a loaf, or into "diamonds," and bake in a hot oven, as long as possible without burning the crust.

FARINA AND GRAHAM BREAD.

Cold boiled farina and wheat-meal may be made into nice bread, in the manner of the preceding recipe. It does not require baking so long.

RYE AND INDIAN BREAD.

Mix two parts corn meal and one part rye-meal ; pour on boiling water enough to wet the whole ; pack it into a pan and steam five or six hours, then set it into the oven to brown. Raisins, dates, currants, or other fruits, may be added to this kind of bread, if desired.

MIXED MEAL BREAD.

Take one part each of rye flour, wheat-meal, and oat-meal, and three parts of corn-meal ; mix thoroughly ; pour on boiling water enough to scald all the meal ; pack into a pan and steam six or seven hours. Before sending to the table it should be browned in the oven. Prunes, raisins, dates or currants may be added to this kind of bread.

PLAIN JOHNNY CAKE.

Wet corn-meal with either hot or cold water, pack it one inch thick in a baking pan, and bake in a hot oven.

PUMPKIN JOHNNY CAKE.

Take pumpkin stewed until it is very dry and sweet, and stir corn meal into it until the mass becomes a rather stiff dough; spread it on a baking pan on which dry meal has been sifted, and bake in a hot oven.

RYE BREAD.

Pour boiling water on rye-flour or rye-meal, and mix into a stiff dough; make it into loaves about three inches in diameter, or cut into squares or rolls, and bake in a hot oven.

OAT-MEAL BREAD.

Take oat-meal mush and knead in dry oat-meal; roll out to the thickness of one quarter of an inch, and cut with a cake cutter, or roll thin as a knife blade; bake as crisps. Boiling water may be poured on the uncooked oat-meal instead of using the mush.

BROWN BREAD.

Scald two parts of corn-meal, let it stand one or two hours; add two parts of rye and one of wheat-meal; mix thoroughly, and as stiff as can be stirred with a strong iron spoon; add raisins or currants if desired, and steam five or six hours; then place it in a moderate oven two hours. It may be served warm or cold.

BREADS.

BERRY SHORT CAKE.

Mix water (the colder the better), wheat-meal, and a little grated cocoanut, so as to form a stiff batter; drop the batter in hot bread pans three-fourths of an inch thick; bake in a hot oven; when cold, split open, lay each half crust down, and cover with ripe strawberries, raspberries, blackberries or whortleberries. Good ripe peaches will answer in place of berries. Any of the fruit sauces, mentioned in another chapter, may be added if desired, on serving the dish.

CORN DODGERS.

Mix corn meal and the coldest water to a stiff dough; mold into small cakes of an oval shape; place in hot pans previously dusted with meal; smooth the top with the hands dipped in water, and bake in a hot oven one hour.

RICE CAKES.

Take two parts of boiled rice, one part of corn meal, and one part of stoned or seedless raisins chopped fine; mix with water to a soft dough, roll into small cakes, and bake in a pan dusted with meal to prevent sticking. It should remain in the oven until a crust is formed.

BERRY TOAST.

Toast thin slices of Graham bread, dip them in hot

water, and cover with hot stewed berries. Blackberries and whortleberries are commonly preferred.

APPLE TOAST.

Apple sauce or stewed apples may be employed in the same manner as berries. If very tart, dates may be used to sweeten.

RHUBARB TOAST.

Peel, and cut the stalks in pieces, put them in a stew pan, add a little water, some stoned dates, and a few English currants well picked and washed; let them all cook until done, and then pour them over the toasted bread.

WHOLE GRAINS AND SEEDS.

These may be roasted over burning coals, or on a hot stove, if placed in a "corn-popper" and shaken constantly; or boiled until soft. Wheat and rice are the favorite grains for boiling, and corn for roasting or "popping."

CHAPTER II.

MUSHES.

GENERAL RULES.

MUSHES of all kinds should be stirred as little as possible while cooking, after the material *sets*, or stops sinking, to the bottom. Much stirring breaks up the particles and frees the starchy matter, rendering the food pasty, and destroying the light, spongy, delicate appearance it should present on the table; too much stirring also makes it more liable to adhere to the bottom of the vessel. The water should boil when the meal or grain is stirred in, be kept boiling, and the mush stirred frequently for a few minutes, when it will cease sinking; then cover closely and cook slowly for an hour or more. Mushes should not be too thick, nor so thin as to spread much on the plate when dished. The tendency of fruit when cooked in mushes is to settle and adhere to the kettle; hence in adding fruit, the better way, as a general rule, is to cook it separately and mix just before dishing. The fruit for this purpose should always be cooked slowly and in as little water as possible.

CRUSHED WHEAT MUSH.

As the grits swell very much in cooking, they should be stirred gradually into boiling water until a thin mush is formed ; the boiling should be contfnued slowly for two or three hours ; the coarser the grits the longer they should be boiled. Raisins may be cooked with it for a seasoning, or stoned dates may be added after it is cooked.

CORN GRITS.

In this market this is prepared from white corn, which is cut into coarser or finer particles of nearly uniform size ; the coarser kind is called *samp*. It is cooked in the same manner as wheaten grits *(crushed wheat—cracked wheat)*, and requires boiling from one to two hours, according to the size of the grits.

HOMINY.

This is very coarse corn grits, the grains of corn being broken into coarse pieces. It should be washed several times ; soaked over night, then boiled in the same water four or five hours. Raisins give this dish a very rich flavor.

FARINA.

This should be gradually stirred into hot water ; a small quantity will cook in half an hour, but larger quantities require boiling slowly one or two hours. Grated cocoanut gives it a fine flavor.

OAT-MEAL MUSH.

Put into your kettle nearly as much water as you wish mush; when it boils stir in the oat-meal evenly until a thin mush is formed; then cover and let it boil slowly half to three-fourths of an hour.

CORN-MEAL MUSH

This is made in the same manner as oat-meal mush, but is improved by longer cooking. The coarser the meal the longer it should be cooked. Very fine meal does not make good mush. English currants or raisins may be cooked with it. Sliced sweet apples may be cooked in it by spreading them near the surface, an hour before it is done.

GRAHAM MUSH.

This is made of Graham-flour (wheat-meal) and hot water, in the same manner as oat-meal mush; but requires cooking only about twenty minutes; care is required in stirring it not to have it lumpy. Stoned dates make the best seasoning.

RYE MUSH.

This is made in the same manner as Graham mush; it is not so palatable as the other mushes.

BERRY MUSH.

Pick and wash the berries; stew them in a little water, adding a few stoned dates, stirring frequently until well cooked; then stir in very evenly a little Graham flour or oat-meal. Blackberries, raspberries, or whortleberries may be used.

RICE MUSH.

Wash the rice and boil it until the grains are soft; do not stir it; when done uncover and let the steam escape. Raisins are the proper fruit when seasoning is desired.

A convenient method of cooking fruited rice mush is, to put the washed rice into a wet bag, filling about one-fourth of it (mixing raisins if desired), and then boil or steam it.

CHAPTER III.

PIES.

GENERAL RULES.

THE chief difficulty in making Hygienic pies is, to have the crust soft and tender without yeast or grease. But this can be done in various ways, and of various materials. But however made and however tender, they can all be rendered still more so by covering them in a stone crock, or, better still, with a few folds of linen cloth, so that the crust will absorb the moisture of the contents. The following recipes for making crust will suit nearly all tastes and circumstances.

GRAHAM PIE CRUST.

Pour boiling water into wheat-meal and stir to a soft dough; roll out as thin as possible; sprinkle a little meal over the pie plate, and spread this as the bottom crust. Make the top crust by mixing wheat-meal with ice-cold water; add grated cocoanut if desired; knead as quickly as possible to a stiff hard dough; roll very thin; cover and bake immediately.

MUSH PIE CRUST.

Take any cold mush—wheat-meal, cold boiled rice, corn-meal, or oat-meal, or any mixture of them; knead a little wheat-meal into it and roll thin, making the upper and under crusts alike. If there is only mush enough for one crust, the top crust may be made according to the preceding recipe.

OAT-MEAL PIE CRUST.

Scald two parts of oat-meal with one part water, and roll thin. This crust bakes very quickly, so that fruit which requires much cooking should be cooked before making into the pie.

POTATO PIE CRUST.

Boil dry mealy potatoes; sift through a colander; mix them thoroughly with one-half the quantity; add boiling water equal to about one-fourth the bulk of the mixture· roll thin, and bake in a moderate oven.

CORN-MEAL PIE CRUST.

A very tender crust for squash, pumpkin, or custard pies, may be made by placing dry corn-meal on the bottom of the dish.

COCOANUT PIE CRUST.

A rich and very delicious pie crust may be made as follows: mix one part grated cocoanut with two parts

Graham flour, and water (the colder the better) sufficient to make a stiff dough; knead five minutes, then add one part of boiled rice and mix thoroughly

APPLE PIE.

Make a crust according to either of the above recipes except the last; spread the bottom crust on the plate; on this spread a few dates, stoned and cut into small pieces; sift a little meal over this, and lay on the apples in slices or stewed; if the fruit is very juicy sift on more meal; cover with the top crust; have the fruit extend close to the edges of the crust, which should be wet so that the top and bottom crust will adhere at their edges; with a knife roll the edges under so that they will be smooth; bake immediately, being careful not to have the top crust much browned. As soon as done, cover tight with a dish about two inches deep, and let it steam till cold, when the crust will be very tender.

BERRY PIE.

This may be made in the same manner as apple pie, using blackberries, raspberries or whortleberries instead of apples. It requires more dates than apple pie does for sweetening, unless the berries are very ripe.

CRANBERRY PIE.

This is also made in the same manner as the preceding, only two or three times the quantity of dates are required. A top crust may be used or not; or narrow strips of a thin crust may be laid across. If no top crust is used it will not need to be covered when done.

RHUBARB PIE.

Peel the stalks and cut into small pieces, putting dates both below and above them.

PUMPKIN PIE.

Stew the pumpkin according to the recipe in this work for so doing; when nearly dry and quite rich, it is ready for the pie. Mix two parts of corn-meal and one part of Graham flour; sift the mixture over a pie plate to the depth of an eighth of an inch; upon this spread a layer of the stewed pumpkin, and on this lay stoned raisins; cover with another layer of pumpkin and bake in a moderate oven. Dates may be used instead of raisins, if preferred. They should be stewed and put through the colander.

STEWED APPLE PIE.

This may be made according to the recipe for pumpkin pie, omitting the top crust.

PEACH PIE.

This is made in the same manner as apple pie.

PEAR PIE.

This may be made in the same manner as the preceding.

DRIED FRUIT PIES.

Nearly all kinds of dried fruits may be made into pies in the same manner as green fruit, first stewing the fruit. It is better to mash the fruit through the colander, and make the pie after the recipe for pumpkin pie.

COCO-CUSTARD PIE.

Make an under crust according to the recipe for cocoanut pie crust, and fill with stewed pumpkin or squash, sweetened with a little date sauce. Other stewed fruits may be used, as apples, peaches, raisins or berries. This pie is improved by the addition of a little lemon juice.

TARTS.

Mix Graham flour plentifully with grated cocoanut; pour into the mixture ice-water enough to make a stiff dough; knead it hard; roll very thin and cut into round cakes two or three inches in diameter; cut out the centre of a part of them, leaving a narrow rim; put three layers of these rims on one centre or round piece, wetting them so as to make them unite; prick the centre with a fork and bake in a quick oven, yet not so as to brown them. They should be crisp and tender when done. When wanted for use they have only to be filled with some kind of fruit sauce, as stewed English currants, pineapple, marmalade, etc.

DUMPLINGS.

Make a crust of wheat-meal, water, and grated cocoanut, thoroughly kneaded as for "Premium Bread;" roll out quickly a small piece of the dough, a little thicker than for pie crust; press it into a tea cup with the hand; fill with sliced tart apples, peaches, whortleberries, or other fruit; press together; bake in a moderate oven one hour, and serve with sauce. Dates and raisins may be employed to sweeten when apples or other tart fruits are used.

CHAPTER IV.

PUDDINGS.

GENERAL RULES.

UDDINGS are intermediate between mushes and pastry. They are substantially baked mushes, or pies with the crust and contents intimately interblended. The principal skill required in producing hygienic puddings, consists in selecting such materials as will, when cooked, present a light spongy mass, and such seasoning ingredients as will render them palatable without impairing their digestivity. Puddings and mushes should always be eaten very slowly and with dry cracker, hard bread, or other solid food, to insure proper mastication.

HYGIENIC BROWN BETTY.

Prepare a quantity of apples for stewing, cleanse some raisins and currants, and stone some dates ; the proportions may be according to taste or fancy ; cut some Graham bread into thin slices ; put into the stewing kettle a layer of the fruits ; then a layer of bread, repeating and alternating until the kettle is nearly full, or until a sufficient quantity is prepared; then pour on cold water until it reaches within two inches of the top of the pudding; set it where it will simmer slowly without burning; cook until the bread and fruit are thoroughly soft, when the liquor will be very rich; serve warm or cold. Grated cocoanut may be added if its flavor is desired.

INDIAN PUDDING.

Prepare apples for stewing, and stone some dates; put Indian-meal into the baking, and pour boiling water into it enough to make a thin mush. Add the apples and dates, grated cocoanut if desired, and bake five or six hours. Raisins and figs may be employed with the other fruits, or instead of them. It may be served with a dressing of stewed English currants, or stewed figs, but is excellent without any sauce.

CORN MUSH PUDDING.

Early in the morning make a mush of corn-meal, stirring it very thick; place it where it will simmer slowly and not burn; let it cook seven or eight hours; an hour before done add as many raisins as may be desired; just before removing from the fire stir in grated cocoanut enough to flavor well; put it into molds to cool. It should be served the next day, with or without a dressing of currant or fig sauce.

SWEET POTATO PUDDING.

Grate half a dozen raw sweet potatoes; mix them with two quarts of green apple juice; add sufficient grated cocoanut to flavor, and raisins if desired; then mix with Graham flour enough ro make a batter of the proper consistency for gems; bake in a pudding dish, or in gem pans. The batter needs beating, and the apple juice should be as cold as possible.

BIRDS' NEST PUDDING.

Put into the bottom of the pudding dish a few stoned raisins; fill two-thirds full with quartered apples—or the apples may be cored whole, and the cavity filled with the raisins; make a batter as for gems, adding grated cocoanut; pour the batter over the apples and bake in a moderate oven. When done loosen the edges of the crust, and turn it upper side down on a plate. Currant sauce is a good dressing.

BAKED APPLE PUDDING.

Boil good apples, with dates enough to sweeten them, in about one-fifth their bulk of water. Put all through a colander; stir in some grated bread crumbs, and a few drops of lemon juice; bake about forty minutes.

SWEET APPLE PUDDING.

Pare and core good ripe sweet apples; fill the centre of each with raisins and cranberries; put them into boiling water into which Indian-meal has been stirred to the consistence of thin mush; bake about three hours. If the apples are not very sweet a few dates will give the requisite flavor, added to the cranberries and raisins.

RICE AND APPLE PUDDING.

Boil the rice until it is soft, half fill the pudding dish with peeled and cored apples whose cavities have been filled with dates; put the rice over the fruit as a crust, and bake one hour.

SNOW-BALL PUDDING.

Pare and core large mellow apples; fill the cavities with dates or raisins; inclose them in cloths spread over with boiled rice; bake one hour. Before turning them out they should be dipped in cold water. Stewed currants or figs make a good sauce for this kind of pudding.

STEAMED PUDDING.

Mix three parts of bread or crackers cut into small pieces, one part tart apples cut in small pieces, and one part dried sweet fruit—raisins, dates, figs, or a mixture of them, chopped fine; add sufficient water to prevent the pudding drying while cooking; mix thoroughly and steam four or five hours, according to quantity.

CHAPTER V.

SAUCES.

GENERAL RULES.

PERSONS whose ideas of sauces as dressings or relishes for food, are limited to combinations of butter, sugar, salt, vinegar, and spices, may be astonished to learn what varieties of wholesome as well as palatable articles can be made by combinations of fruits and their juices. The number is practically unlimited, but Hygienists usually have or soon acquire appetences so nearly normal that they are satisfied with few. All that is required to make a wholesome and palatable sauce or dressing, is a selection of fruits that are themselves wholesome, and such admixtures and preparations of them as will suit the taste. The following recipes are favorite specimens.

COCOANUT SAUCE.

Stew equal parts of chopped figs, raisins and English currants for an hour in water sufficient to cover them; when nearly done add grated cocoanut in quantity to suit the taste, and a little Graham flour to thicken. An excellent sauce may be made by adding grated cocoa-nut to date sauce.

DATE SAUCE.

Boil the dates for an hour, or until tender, in water enough to cover them; sift through a colander, rejecting such portions as will not pass; stir thoroughly, adding more water if too thick, and boil again; if too sweet acid fruit of any kind, boiled and passed through a colander, may be added before it is boiled the last time. Dried or canned fruits may be used with the dates; or the juices of canned fruits may be added without passing through the colander.

LEMON SAUCE.

This is made in the same manner as date sauce, omitting all fruits, except the dates, and adding the grated peel of lemon sufficient for the flavor desired. Grate the peel before the lemon is cut, and care should be taken to grate only the yellow part, as the white part is bitter and indigestible.

APPLE AND TOMATO SAUCE.

Boil good ripe tomatoes, which have been scalded and peeled, fifteen to twenty minutes; then add an equal quantity of sliced apples, and cook until the apples are soft.

SAUCES. 37

DRIED FRUIT SAUCE.

All kinds of fruit, or mixtures of them, cooked until well done and properly thinned with water, make good dressings, or sauces for puddings and mushes.

GRAPE AND APPLE SAUCE.

Equal parts of stewed grapes and sweet apples, strained through a thin cloth, and thickened with a little rice or Graham flour, make a rich sauce for rice, hominy, samp, and other mushes. Sour apples and dates may be used instead of sweet apples.

ORANGE SAUCE.

This is made in the same manner as the above, substituting orange for lemon, and adding some acid fruit when the orange juice is not sufficiently tart.

CURRANT SAUCE.

Pick and wash English currants very carefully, then stew a few minutes, and serve cold.

FIG SAUCE.

Wash the figs; chop them coarse, and stew in water enough to make the sauce of the requisite consistence.

SAUCE FOR SHORT CAKE.

Stew dates and rub them through a colander; set the liquid over the fire, and when boiling thicken with a little Graham flour or farina, wet with berry juice. Or chop figs into small pieces; stew in a small quantity of water; strain, and it is ready for use.

This sauce is intended specially for strawberry short-cake, but will answer for berry cakes of all kinds.

NOTE.—The above sauces or dressings may be used indiscriminately with crushed wheat, rice, hominy, oat-meal, all kinds of mushes, steamed puddings, berry cakes, etc. Either of them is an excellent relish for any dish for which any dressing is desired; but we have indicated such preferences as experience in providing for a great variety of tastes and habits has suggested.

CHAPTER VI.

SOUPS.

GENERAL RULES.

HYGIENIC soups consist of one or more vegetables boiled very soft, and equally diffused through a large proportion of water. If eaten with bread, cracker, uncooked fruit, or other solid food, they are not objectionable as slop food. They are usually made of varying proportions of potatoes, peas, beans, carrots, turnips, beets, parsnips, etc., and sometimes flavored with tomatoes. The following varieties are favorites with us.

VEGETABLE SOUP.

Take three medium-sized turnips, a small head of cabbage, four or five medium-sized carrots, three medium-sized parsnips, and three quarts of pared potatoes; chop all of the vegetables except the potatoes very fine; put them in three quarts of water; boil them till nearly done; then add the potatoes and cook until they are reduced to a pulp. A small quantity of tomatoes may be added, or not, as preferred. Beans and peas added to vegetable soup increases its richness.

TOMATO SOUP.

Scald and peel good ripe tomatoes; stew them one hour; strain through a coarse sieve; add grated potatoes to thicken sufficiently, and cook half an hour longer.

SPLIT PEA SOUP.

Wash one pint of split peas, and boil in three quarts of water three hours.

BEAN SOUP.

Wash the beans; put them in cold water and raise the temperature slowly to the boiling point; add water enough to have the soup of the thickness desired; boil until the beans are softened; press them through a colander, and boil for a minute or two. Sago, soaked, may then be added if desired.

GREEN BEAN SOUP.

Boil one quart of garden or kidney beans, and put them through the colander; add an equal quantity of vegetable broth; dredge in a little Graham flour or oatmeal; stir the dish until it boils; then add one ounce of spinach and one ounce of parsley, chopped fine; scald till these are done, and send to the table.

GREEN PEA SOUP.

Take three pints of peas; three medium-sized turnips, one carrot, and the pods of the peas; boil one quart of the largest of the peas with the pods until they are quite soft; rub them through a fine colander: return the pulp into the pan; add the turnips, the carrot, sliced, and a quart of boiling water; when the vegetables are nearly soft, add the smaller peas. Potatoes may be used instead of turnips.

SPINACH SOUP.

Take two quarts of spinach, half a pound of parsley, two carrots, two turnips, and one root of celery; stew all of them in a pint of water until quite soft; rub them through a coarse sieve; add one quart of hot water and boil them twenty minutes.

VEGETABLE AND RICE SOUP.

Take one pound of turnips, half a pound of carrots, one-fourth of a pound of parsnips, half a pound of potatoes, and three tablespoonsful of rice; chop the vegetables fine; put the turnips, carrots, and parsnips into a pan with a quart of boiling water; add the rice; boil them one hour; add the potatoes and two quarts of water, and boil them until they are all well done.

POTATO SOUP.

Wash and pare, but do not cut, the potatoes, put them in a little more than enough of boiling water to cover them; if any lumps remain after boiling pass them through a colander. This soup is as delicious as it is simple, and is always a favorite with Hygienists.

ASPARAGUS SOUP.

Prepare asparagus as for boiling in the ordinary manner; cut the tender part of the stalks into small pieces; add half the quantity of potatoes, and cook till a thick soup is formed. This is a favorite and delicious dish.

VEGETABLE BROTH.

This may be made of various combinations and proportions of the vegetables used in making soups, to suit different tastes or fancies. The following recipe will serve as a basis. Take four turnips, two carrots, one onion, and a spoonful of lentil flour. Cut the vegetables in pieces, and boil all the ingredients together until well cooked, in water sufficient to make a thin soup.

BARLEY BROTH.

Take four ounces of pearl barley; two turnips, and three ounces of corn-meal; steep the barley (after being washed) twelve hours; put it on the fire in five quarts of water; add the turnips chopped fine; boil one hour; stir in the meal; thin if necessary with more water, and let it simmer gently twenty minutes.

PORRIDGES.

These are thin mushes. Oat-meal is the favorite article for porridge; but wheat-meal makes a good dish. The following recipe will serve for all dishes of this kind. Stir one-fourth of a pound of oat-meal into a little cold water until the mixture is smooth and uniform; add one pint of boiling water, and boil twenty minutes.

GRUELS.

These are thin porridges. They may be made in the same manner, adding two or three times as much water. They are seldom used except for fever patients. Wheat-meal and corn-meal make the best dishes.

CHAPTER VII.

VEGETABLES.

GENERAL RULES.

ALL boiled vegetables should be cooked in as ltttle water as possible; the secret of procuring the richest flavor and best quality of boiled vegetable food consists in using just water enough to have it nearly evaporated when the vegetables are done. The water should be boiling when the vegetables are put in it and raised to the boiling point as soon as possible afterwards. With few exceptions all edible vegetables are more wholesome as well as nutritive when fully ripe. The principal exceptions are, peas, beans, corn, cucumbers and spinach, which may be eaten at any stage of growth. The fresher they are the better always. The cook who would economize fuel and labor should know that boiling is a process that cannot be hurried. If the water is kept at the boiling point nothing more can be done to hurry the cooking. Any additional heat is lost in steam. All vessels in which vegetables are boiled should be kept clean and bright. In baking potatoes it is important that those of nearly uniform size be selected, if all are to be placed on the table at the same time. Probably no common article of food is more abused by the agriculturist and maltreated by the cook, than the potato. And we commend to all who would understand the culture, preservation, and best method of using this important tuber, a little work by Dr. John McLaurin, entitled the "Model Potato."*

MODEL COOKED POTATOES.

Select potatoes of uniform size; wash quickly in cold water, without cutting; put them in a kettle or tight-lidded saucepan, filling the vessel about two-thirds full; cover tightly, and cook them in their own juices. They should be put in an oven or over a fire sufficiently hot to convert the water they contain into steam. As soon as softened they can be peeled and placed on the table, or served with their skins on. Cooked in this manner potatoes have a richness of flavor unknown to any other method.

BOILED POTATOES.

Wash in cold water without cutting; cover them with water, and boil in a covered vessel until soft enough to be readily penetrated with a fork; pour off the water; shake them up loosely, and let them remain uncovered to dry. Some kinds of potatoes have a richer flavor when cooked with the skins on.

* For sale by S. R. Wells. Price 50 cents.

BOILED PEELED POTATOES.

Wash, pare, and put them in cold water; if old they are improved by soaking several hours; then boil them in water just sufficient to cover them, the kettle being uncovered; as soon as the fork will readily pass through them, pour off the water, shake them up loosely, and let them remain uncovered a few minutes. This method renders them dry and mealy.

MASHED POTATOES.

Wash, pare and boil the potatoes according to the preceding recipe; when tender pour off the water and mash them until smooth and destitute of lumps; then beat them with a fork until they are light and white, and send to the table, not pressed down, but laid in the dish lightly.

BROWNED POTATOES.

Take cold boiled potatoes, cut them in thin slices; lay them on a gridiron; place them over the fire, or on a tin in a hot oven; if the latter, put them first on the bottom so that the under side will brown and the moisture escape; then change them to the upper grate to brown the upper side. Send them immediately to the table.

BROWNED MASHED POTATOES.

Take cold mashed potatoes; compress them into a dish, smoothing the top; place them in a hot oven till warmed thoroughly through, and browned on the top. An elegant dish may be made by forming the mashed potatoes into small cones two and a half inches high, placing them on a pan, and browning quickly in a hot oven.

BAKED POTATOES.

If the potatoes to be baked are all to be served at the same time, it is very important that they are of nearly uniform size. They require a hot oven, and as soon as done, the skin of each should be broken to let out the vapor, then served immediately.

ROASTED POTATOES.

Wash them carefully; cover with hot ashes, and when done they will be very rich and mealy.

STEAMED POTATOES.

In cooking potatoes by steam, the steam should be generated before putting the potatoes into the steaming vessel, and kept up briskly afterwards until they are done. It will render them more dry and mealy to take off the cover just before they are done, or put them in an oven to dry and finish.

SWEET POTATOES.

These may be baked or boiled with their skins on. When boiled they should be peeled before sending to the table. They may be par-boiled, then peeled and browned in the oven. They are excellent if sliced and browned the next day after being boiled.

MASHED SWEET POTATOES.

Sweet potatoes may be boiled and mashed, or mashed and browned in the manner mentioned for white potatoes.

BOILED TURNIPS.

Wash and peel the turnips; put them in just boiling water enough to cook them and be evaporated by the time they are soft. They may be sent to the table whole, sliced or mashed. A little potato added and mashed with them makes a nice dish.

BROWNED TURNIPS.

These are very palatable when prepared of cold boiled turnips in the same manner as mashed or sliced potatoes. Early turnips are best, when cooked dry and mashed.

BOILED BEETS.

Wash the beets without cutting. The tops and fibrous roots should be twisted off instead of cut, so as not to waste the juice; they may be boiled like turnips, or steamed like potatoes; a large kettle full requires boiling steadily four or five hours. When very tender place them in cold water and remove the skins; then slice immediately and send to the table. Beets may also be baked like potatoes.

CHOPPED BEETS AND TOMATOES.

Chop very tenderly cooked beets very fine ; mix them with an equal quantity of canned or stewed tomatoes ; boil them together a few minutes, and send to the table.

BOILED PARSNIPS.

Wash the parsnips, scrape their skins off, and if large cut them in pieces; put them into boiling water and cook till very tender. It is well to have all the water evaporate in the process of cooking, and if they are browned a little on the bottom of the kettle it will add to the richness of their flavor. When stewed until the liquor becomes rich and sweet, this should be served with the parsnips.

BROWNED PARSNIPS.

Cold boiled parsnips, sliced and browned in the same manner as potatoes, make an excellent relish with breakfast.

CARROTS.

These may be boiled and browned in the same manner as parsnips and potatoes. They require longer cooking than parsnips, and to most persons are much less palatable.

BOILED CABBAGE.

Take off the outer leaves ; cut the head in quarters or half-quarters ; cook in as small a quantity of water as possible until thoroughly done. It should be cooked in a tightly-covered kettle.

CABBAGE AND TOMATOES.

Chop the cabbage fine ; place it in a kettle with very little water, and cover tightly ; let the moisture nearly evaporate, and when nearly done, add one half the quantity of canned or stewed tomatoes ; cook thoroughly, being careful not to burn the mixture.

CAULIFLOWER.

Cut off the green leaves ; cleanse the heads carefully from insects ; then boil in water just sufficient to be evaporated when the article is tender.

ASPARAGUS.

Put the stalks into cold water ; cut off all that is very tough ; then peel and tie the stalks in a bundle or bundles ; boil fifteen to twenty minutes, or until tender ; lift them on the dish, remove the string, and send to the table.

GREENS.

Under this head are comprised spinach, beet-tops, cabbage-sprouts, turnip-leaves, mustard-leaves, all of which are excellent, and milk-weed leaves, cowslips, and dandelion leaves, which, though a trifle bitter, are not unwholesome. All require to be carefully washed and cleaned, and boiled until very tender; then drained in a colander and sent to the table.

GREEN PEAS.

These are much richer in flavor if gathered just before being cooked; do not wash the pods unless necessary; shell and cook immediately in just water enough to make a rich sweet gravy with them.

When very young and tender it improves them to wash the pods and then scald them in the water in which the peas are to be cooked; then remove the pods and add the peas; when cooked they will have a sweeter flavor, derived from the juices of the pods.

GREEN BEANS.

When very young the pods need only to be clipped, cut finely, and boiled in as little water as possible until tender; when older, break off the ends and strip off the strings that line their edges; break them into small pieces, and boil until tender. They require boiling three or four hours.

BOILED GREEN CORN.

Trim off the husks and silk; put the ears in hot water, and boil them twenty or thirty minutes; or the ears may be steamed one-half to three-fourths of an hour. The kernels may be cut from the cob, scraping the cob after cutting, a little hot water added, and cooked by boiling ten or fifteen minutes.

ROASTED GREEN CORN.

Remove the husks and silk; place the ears on a gridiron, and this over red hot coals or in a hot oven.

SUCCOTASH.

This is usually made of green corn and garden beans, though string beans are sometimes added. Cut the corn from the cobs, scraping them afterwards; add the beans and a trifle of hot water; cover closely and boil until the beans are soft. Lima beans and sugar corn make an excellent succotash.

GARDEN BEANS.

Shell the beans from the pod; add a very little water, and cook until the beans are very tender and the juice thickened.

LIMA BEANS.

These should be cooked in the same manner as garden beans.

BOILED DRIED BEANS.

Wash the beans thoroughly, and put them in a kettle

of cold water; let them be heated slowly to the boiling point, and cooked until done—about three hours. Do not parboil them. It is a mistaken notion that the first water is injurious. It removes much of the richness of the bean to turn off the water. It is well to let them soak over night, first washing them, and then cooking them in the water in which they have been soaked.

BAKED DRIED BEANS.

Prepare them as for boiling; boil them nearly soft, place them in the baking pan, with a part of the water, and let them bake in the oven until moderately browned.

MASHED BAKED BEANS.

Prepare them according to the preceding recipe, only a little drier; then with a spoon or pestle mash them to a powder and bake. This is a delicious dish.

BEANS AND CABBAGE.

When the beans are half boiled, add a head of cabbage, cut into small pieces. Beans and potatoes may be mixed in the same manner.

SPLIT PEAS.

Pick them over carefully and wash thoroughly; put them over the fire in cold water; adding hot water as they become dry; they may be cooked nearly dry, or more moist, as preferred. They require cooking about two hours. They may be baked in the same manner as beans. When cold they may be sliced and browned, making a nice breakfast dish.

DRIED GREEN PEAS.

Pick over and wash thoroughly; soak them over night in soft water; in the morning put them over the fire in the water in which they have been soaked; boil three hours and a half, or until tender. These may be baked in the same manner as beans.

CUCUMBERS.

These require no cooking. They are not objectionable to healthy stomachs, nor to most invalids, if eaten fresh as a part of the meal. If kept any time they should be placed in the refrigerator, or in cold water

CHAPTER VIII.

FRUITS.

GENERAL RULES.

THE majority of good ripe fruits cannot be improved by cooking, provided they are to constitute a principal or even large proportion of the meal; nevertheless they can be cooked in many ways without impairing their wholesomeness, and rendering some of them more acceptable to invalid stomachs, as well as agreeable to tastes variously cultivated, and more or less vitiated. Fruits may be baked, steamed, boiled, or stewed, the only rules to be observed being, to cook them uniformly until soft, and not scorch or burn them. We give a list of our favorite recipes. Fruits should be cooked in stone or porcelain vessels, not in tin, brass, or copper.

BAKED APPLES.

Select apples of nearly uniform size; fill the baking plate with them, pour on a few spoonsful of water, and cook till softened all through.

BAKED APPLES WITH DATES.

Take large tart apples; pare and core them whole; fill the place of the core with dates; place them in the baking plate, pour over them a little water, and cook till softened through.

BAKED PARED APPLES.

Pare, quarter, and core the apples; fill the pudding dish with them; if very tart distribute a few pieces of dates among them; if very juicy add no water, if not add a little; bake and place them in a cool place.

STEAMED APPLES.

For steaming apples should be prepared as for baking. About twice as much time is required as for baking.

STEWED APPLES.

Apples may be stewed whole, or with the skins or cores, or both removed. They certainly have a richer flavor when cooked with the skins on. When quite tart a few dates may be cooked with them. A very nice and delicious dish is made by passing stewed apples through a colander, beating them until light and spongy, and placing them in a pudding dish, to be moderately browned in the oven.

FRUITS. 57

STEWED DRIED APPLES.

Pick over the fruit carefully, reject all imperfect or discolored pieces; wash thoroughly; then boil in just water enough to cover them. They may be flavored with proper proportions of dried peaches, raisins, figs, dates, or quinces.

PEARS.

Pears may be baked, boiled, or stewed, in the same manner as apples. Some varieties of small early pears are very delicious when boiled whole without paring, or stewed a long time with a few dates among them.

As pears are among the most perishable of fruits, they may be picked before they are quite ripe, and placed in a dry cool place to ripen. A favorite method with us of cooking such pears is, to pare, halve and core them, and stew in sufficient water to make a rich juice, adding a few figs to flavor. Send the dish cold to the table.

PEACHES.

The idea of cooking good ripe peaches is never to be entertained. But those of inferior quality, or those not fully ripe, may be improved by boiling them. They should be peeled, except when the skins are very smooth, clean and tender. They should not be stoned. Figs are the best seasonings, and should be cut in pieces and cooked with them.

STEWED DRIED PEACHES.

Dried peaches (or dried pears when obtainable) may be stewed in the same manner as dried apples. A nice dish may be prepared by cooking them rather dry, mashing them through a colander, placing the pulp on a pie plate, and baking moderately in the oven.

APRICOTS.

Apricots are to be prepared and used in the same manner as peaches.

QUINCES.

Quinces are of little value *per se*, but when dried or canned, are excellent to flavor other fruits with.

PINEAPPLES.

The remarks in relation to quinces are equally applicable to pineapples.

CRANBERRIES.

Pick and wash the berries; add dates enough to sweeten to suit the taste; stew in as little water as possible without burning them until they become soft; then mash the whole through a colander and set away to cool.

BLACKBERRIES.

Ripe and rich-flavored blackberries neither admit of

nor require cooking. But when the fruit is unripe or inferior, it should be cooked. Pick over the fruit, and wash if necessary; put it into a stew kettle with a very little water; if very sour add a few dates; boil fifteen minutes; serve cold.

WHORTLEBERRIES.

When not fully ripe these may be cooked in the same manner as blackberries.

RASPBERRIES.

The same remarks apply to these berries.

STRAWBERRIES.

When not fully ripe, strawberries, for invalids, should be stewed with a few dates, taking care not to have them very juicy. When ripe and clean, no cooking, preparation, or seasoning can improve them. If sandy or dirty they should be quickly rinsed in cold water before serving. An ornamental dish may be prepared by putting a layer of green leaves around the edge of the dish, and filling it with the hulled berries.

CHERRIES.

When too sour or not sufficiently ripe to eat without cooking or seasoning, cherries may be stewed and sweetened with dates.

PLUMS.

There are many varieties of plums, some of which are sweet and luscious, while others are sour and unpalatable. They are to be managed in the same manner as cherries.

CURRANTS.

Green currants are not unwholesome when stewed and sweetened with dates. When fully ripe they are good without cooking.

GOOSEBERRIES.

These may be managed in the same manner as currants.

BANANAS.

These are not *cookable*. They should be peeled, sliced, and eaten with bread, rice, or mushes.

ORANGES.

These may be put on the table whole, or peeled and the sections separated.

LEMONS.

We only use lemons to flavor sauces, pies, puddings, greens, etc.

TOMATOES.

Very ripe tomatoes are better uncooked. But if imperfectly ripened they should be stewed in as little water as possible and for a long time. They may be cooked in half an hour, but will improve if stewed one or even two hours longer. Crumbs or pieces of toasted bread are an excellent addition; or the juice may be thickened with a little Graham flour.

MELONS.

None of the numerous varieties of watermelons and muskmelons can be improved by cooking. They should not be taken from the vines till fully ripe, and the sooner after being gathered they are eaten, the more wholesome and delicious.

RHUBARB.

This is prepared as for making pie, and stewed with dates to sweeten.

PUMPKINS.

Some of the richer kinds of pumpkins are good if baked; but all are excellent when properly stewed or steamed. As little water as possible without allowing the pumpkin to burn should be used. Like tomatoes, pumpkin is rendered richer and sweeter by prolonged cooking. When nearly done it should be left uncovered, to evaporate some of the water.

SQUASH.

Stewing is the usual method of cooking all kinds of squashes; but some of the more solid and richer kinds are excellent and sometimes preferable when baked. Wash, wipe, cut in four or more pieces, remove the seeds, and bake in a pan. Steaming squash, however, is better than boiling it.

GRAPES.

The idea of cooking rich ripe grapes is inadmissible; if sour or not fully ripe, they may be stewed in as little water as possible, and pressed through a colander to remove the skin and seeds.

PRUNES.

Stew them until soft in just water enough to cover them; do not stir them so as to mangle the skins; they should appear on the table plump and unbroken.

ENGLISH DRIED CURRANTS.

These are generally used to flavor ether dishes, but are excellent of themselves; they may be stewed in the same manner as most other dried fruits.

FIGS.

When quite fresh, figs are better uncooked; when old

they should be quickly washed in boiling water, and then stewed until soft.

DATES.

These may be eaten uncooked with other foods; but we seldom use them except to sweeten and flavor other fruits and foods.

CHAPTER IX.

PRESERVING FOODS.

GENERAL RULES.

ANNING, drying, and refrigeration are the only hygienic processes for preserving fruits, vegetables, or foods of any kind. Antiseptics of every sort—salt, sugar, vinegar, alcohol, etc., not only add injurious ingredients, but change the organic arrangement of the constituent molecules, deteriorate the quality of the food, and lessen its nutritive value.

The process of canning has reached great perfection within a few years, so that almost all kinds of fruits and vegetables can be preserved in their natural flavors for an indefinite time, without a particle of sugar or salt. All that is required is a perfect expulsion of atmospheric air, and its complete exclusion afterwards. Some articles require heating to the boiling point, and others considerable cooking in order to expel all the air.

Of the various jars for canning, the best are "Masons,"

the "Gem," and the "Hero." These are all of glass, and for fruits no other material should be employed.

Within a few years great improvements have been made in drying fruits and vegetables. And the recent introduction of "Boswell's Heater and Dryer" seems to be all that can be desired for families to dry any food they wish to preserve in that manner, economically and in perfection.

The objections to drying in the sun is the exposure of the articles to dust and insects, while drying over a range or in an oven is troublesome and expensive. Some of the methods for drying which have been introduced and patented, although rapid and economical, do not well preserve the nutritive value and natural flavor of the articles. Some of them are so arranged that the steam or vapor which is evaporated from the lower tiers or layers passes through those above, thus *cooking out* and dissipating their juices and flavor. This is obviated in "Boswell's Heater and Dryer." This is so arranged that a current of fresh air carries the moisture of each layer into the flue, producing an article which for flavor, richness, color, and nutritive value, cannot probably be excelled. As the Heater is useful also in drying clothes, heating rooms, and in cooking victuals, every family which has fruit to dry will find it doubly economical; and it would pay many who do not raise fruit, to purchase in season and dry for themselves in Boswell's Heater.

Fruits for canning should be carefully selected, and all

imperfect, decayed, or unripe ones rejected. When sandy or unclean they should be quickly and carefully washed. Blackberries, raspberries, and whortleberries, are canned without difficulty so as to keep well. Strawberries require longer cooking and more careful management. Grapes, cherries, currants, and all of the staple fruits are successfully canned with little trouble.

BERRIES.

Cover them with a little water in a stewing kettle; boil for a few minutes, being careful not to have them burned; fill the jar with them while boiling hot; wipe the edges of the jars clean; screw down the top tight, and put them in a cool place. Do not let a draught of cold air strike them, or they may break. The jar for receiving the fruit should be clean and hot. A convenient method of heating it is to place it sidewise into hot water, (being careful that the water enters the inside the moment it touches the outside, or the vessel may crack), give it a whirl, lift it out and let the water run out, set it in a pan over the stove or in a warm place, and fill immediately. When stone jars are employed for canning, place them on the stove, with a little cold water in them, some time before commencing to cook the fruit. When the water in them is heated nearly to the boiling point, they may be emptied and filled with the hot fruit. The cork should fit closely, and be covered with cement. This may be made of sealing-wax and bees-wax, or of resin and bees-wax; the proportions of sealing-wax and bees-wax should be such that the cement when cold will be neither sticky nor brittle. The cement should be melted and poured over the corks instantly after they are applied to the jars. The jars should be watched until cold, and if any air-bubbles appear in the cement, prick them and add more cement.

STRAWBERRIES.

As these berries are exceptional, we give a special recipe. Boil the fruit thirty minutes after filling the jars in the manner above mentioned, let them stand five minutes to settle; fill the shrinkage, seal tight, and turn the jars on their top; let them remain in this position over night; the next morning the imperfect ones can be detected and corrected.

GRAPES.

Canned grapes are admissable with mushes and puddings in the winter season, or as a relish with any kind of farinaceous food at all seasons. Select the freshest, nicest bunches, and can in the usual manner. An excellent jelly for farinaceous dishes may be prepared by stewing the grapes, mashing them through a colander to remove the skins and seeds, and then canning in the usual manner.

PACKING GRAPES.

Grapes may be easily preserved in the following manner: Take the late grapes; pick them carefully; spread them out in a cool place in layers on shelves; let them remain two weeks; then pack them in barrels with dry hard-wood sawdust. Bran will answer very well. Packed in this manner the fruit will keep good through the winter. After packing they should be kept in a cool and dry place.

Grapes may be kept in good condition for several weeks, by dipping the end of the stem of perfect bunches in melted sealing-wax, then wrapping the bunches in tissue paper, and laying or suspending them in a dry cool place. The more paper that is placed between them the longer they will keep.

APPLES.

Peel, quarter, core, and stew until soft; then can them in the same manner as berries.

PEACHES.

In order to preserve their color, peaches after being peeled should be kept in cold water, until you are ready to can them. They are canned in the same manner as berries. They may be canned with or without peeling and stoning. It is important that they are boiling hot when sealed, and that all of the fruit is covered by its juices.

PEARS.

These may be treated in the same manner as peaches. If gathered before they are quite ripe, they may be laid away in a dry, cool place to ripen, and then canned.

TOMATOES.

Those of the firmest flesh, or least juicy, are the best for canning; cover them with hot water; remove the skins and cut away all the green part; then stew and can in the usual manner. This fruit may be improved by much cooking before canning. There is no objection to tin cans for preserving tomatoes, if they are new; and the fruit is more easily kept in them, as they can be hermetically sealed without difficulty.

RHUBARB.

Peel the rhubarb; stew with dates enough to sweeten as desired, and can in the usual manner.

BANANAS.

This fruit may be canned in the usual manner. It makes an admirable sweetening and flavoring ingredient for pies.

VEGETABLES.

Green corn, peas, beans, and asparagus, are preserved by canning with more difficulty than are most kinds of fruits; hence nearly all the canning establishments add more or less sugar, salt, or some other antiseptic. But this is entirely unnecessary. If well cooked and managed in all respects in the manner recommended for strawberries, there need be no difficulty in keeping them fresh and sweet the year round.

NOTE.—A Miss Jones, of New York, has invented a method of canning fruit in their own juices without cooking them, which is said to be a labor-saving and economical improvement on all existing methods of canning. It consists in removing the air from the fruit and vessel holding it, filling the vacuum by infiltrating the juices of other fruit, previously prepared, and then sealing. Considerable machinery is required for this process, and we hope she will soon have it so perfected and cheapened that it may come into general use.

INDEX.

	PAGE		PAGE
APPLE and Tomato Sauce	36	Corn-meal Pie Crust	26
Apple Bread	16	Corn Mush Pudding	32
Apple Pie	27	Cranberries	58
Apple Toast	20	Cranberry Pie	27
Apricots	58	Crushed Wheat Mush	22
Asparagus	50	Cucumbers	54
Asparagus Soup	42	Currants	60
		Currant Sauce	37
BAKED Apple Pudding	33		
Baked Apples	55	**D**ATES	63
Baked Apples with Dates	56	Date Sauce	36
Baked Dried Beans	53	Dried Fruit Pie	29
Baked Pared Apples	56	Dried Fruit Sauce	37
Baked Potatoes	47	Dried Green Peas	54
Bananas	60	Dumplings	30
Barley Broth	42		
Beans and Cabbage	53	**E**NGLISH Dried Currants	62
Bean Soup	40		
Berry Mush	24	**F**ANCY Breads	16
Berry Pie	27	Farina	22
Berry Short-cake	19	Farina and Graham Bread	17
Berry Toast	19	Figs	62
Birds' Nest Pudding	33	Fig Sauce	37
Blackberries	58	Fruit Bread	14
Boiled Beets	48	Fruit Gems	13
Boiled Cabbage	50	Fruits	55
Boiled Dried Beans	52		
Boiled Green Corn	51	**G**ARDEN Beans	52
Boiled Peeled Potatoes	46	Gems	12
Boiled Potatoes	45	Gooseberries	60
Boiled Parsnips	49	Graham Mush	23
Boiled Turnips	48	Graham Pie Crust	25
Breads	9	Grape and Apple Sauce	37
Brown Bread	18	Grapes	62
Browned Mashed Potatoes	46	Green Beans	51
Browned Parsnips	49	Green Bean Soup	40
Browned Potatoes	46	Green Peas	51
Browned Turnips	48	Green Pea Soup	40
		Greens	50
CABBAGE and Tomatoes	50	Gruels	43
Carrots	49		
Cauliflower	50	**H**OMINY	22
Cherries	59	Hot Water Loaf Bread	12
Chopped Beets and Tomatoes	49	Hot Water Rolls	12
Cocoa-Custard	29	Hygienic Brown Betty	31
Cocoanut Bread	14		
Cocoanut Pie Crust	26	**I**NDIAN Pudding	32
Cocoanut Sauce	35		
Cold Water Loaf Bread	11	**J**OHNNY Cake	17
Corn and Graham Bread	16		
Corn Dodgers	19	**L**EMONS	60
Corn Grits	22	Lemon Sauce	36
Corn-meal Mush	23	Lima Beans	52

INDEX.

MASHED Baked Beans	53
Mashed Potatoes	46
Mashed Sweet Potatoes	48
Melons	61
Mixed Meal Bread	17
Model Cooked Potatoes	45
Mushes	21
Mush Pie Crust	26
Mush Rolls	12
OAT-MEAL Bread	18
Oat-meal Crisps	14
Oat-meal Mush	23
Oat-meal Pie Crust	26
Oranges	60
Orange Sauce	37
PEACHES	57
Peach Pie	28
Pear Pie	29
Pears	57
Pies	25
Pineapple	58
Plain Johnny Cake	17
Plums	60
Porridges	43
Potato Pie Crust	26
Potato Soup	41
Premium Bread	10
Preserving Fruits	64
Prunes	62
Puddings	31
Pumpkin Bread	16
Pumpkin Johnny Cake	18
Pumpkin Pie	28
Pumpkins	61
QUINCES	58
RASPBERRIES	59
Rice	24
Rice and Apple Pudding	34
Rice Cakes	19
Rhubarb	61
Rhubarb Pie	28

Rhubarb Toast	20
Roasted Green Corn	52
Roasted Potatoes	47
Rye and Indian Bread	17
Rye Bread	18
Rye Mush	23
SAUCES	35
Short-cake Sauce	37
Snow Ball Pudding	34
Snow Bread	16
Soups	39
Spinach Soup	41
Split Peas	53
Split Pea Soup	40
Squash	62
Steamed Apples	56
Steamed Potatoes	47
Steamed Pudding	34
Stewed Apple Pie	28
Stewed Apples	56
Stewed Dried Apples	57
Stewed Dried Peaches	57
Strawberries	59
Succotash	62
Sweet Apple Pudding	33
Sweet Potato Bread	15
Sweet Potatoes	47
Sweet Potato Fruit Bread	15
Sweet Potato Pudding	33
TARTS	29
Tomatoes	61
Tomato Soup	40
VEGETABLE and Rice Soup	41
Vegetables	44
Vegetable Broth	42
Vegetable Soup	39
WHEAT-MEAL Crisps	13
White Potato Bread	15
Whole Grains and Seeds	20
Whortleberries	59

F. E. SMITH & CO.'S
Crushed
WHITE WHEAT,
AND
Superlative Graham,

The most excellent and popular preparations of WHOLE WHEAT now manufactured.

Sold by all Grocers,

In Packages of 2, 6 and 12 Lbs.

Pamphlets, containing testimonials, receipts, and other valuable information.

ATLANTIC FLOUR MILLS,

18, 20 and 22 Hamilton Ave.,

BROOKLYN, N. Y.

HECKERS' FARINA.

A very agreeable, light, nutritive food, a superior article for **PUDDINGS** and **JELLIES**, and highly recommended by physicians for invalids and children. As a food for infants, it is, beyond doubt, the best that can be substituted for the nourishment received from the mother.

Heckers' Cracked Wheat.

The most popular preparation of wheat for producing and maintaining a healthful, active condition of the system. It contains, in a larger proportion than most other articles of food, the Phosphates and Nitrogenous elements so necessary to the perfect development of muscle, nerve, and brain, and is peculiarly beneficial to dyspeptics and persons of sedentary habits.

HECKERS' SUPERLATIVE FLOUR

Received the First Premiums at the World's Fair, London; the World's Fair, New York; and wherever exhibited, both in Europe and America. It is very popular with those desiring the finest bread or biscuit that can be produced.

Hecker's **Croton, Manhattan,** and **Magnolia Brands,** so long and favorably known, still maintain their high reputation for uniformity and excellence of quality, and are very popular with those desiring choice pastry or family flour.

HECKERS' GRAHAM FLOUR

Is made from first quality white wheat, and has no superior in the market.

FOR SALE BY ALL GROCERS,
OR AT THE
CROTON MILLS,
203 Cherry Street, New York.

THE
Mother's Hygienic Hand-Book,

For the Normal Development and Training of Women and Children, and the Treatment of their Diseases with Hygienic Agencies. By R. T. TRALL, M.D., author of "The Hydropathic Encyclopedia," "The True Healing Art," "Digestion and Dyspepsia," etc. One vol., 12mo. Plain $1. Fine ed. $1.25. New York: S. R. WELLS, 389 Broadway, Publisher.

This is the latest and the best of the author's many excellent works. It covers ground the most important. It has to do with the perpetuation of the race. Shall children be well or illy gener ted ? Shall the lives of mothers be imperiled while perform ng the functions of motherhood ? Or may she, by certain information given in this HAND-BOOK, pass through the trying periods without danger and with but trifling pain ? Yea, verily, it may—and it *must*—be even so. Among other important matters not named here, this MOTHER'S HYGIENIC HAND-BOOK contains:

CHAPTER	CHAPTER
I. Ante-Natal Influences.	XII. Management of Labor.
II. Anatomy of the Uterine System.	XIII. Attentions to the Child.
III. Displacements of the Uterus.	XIV. Attentions to the Mother.
IV. Menstruation—Regular.	XV. Disorders Incident to Labor.
V. Menstrual Disorders.	XVI. Disorders During Lactation.
VI. Pregnancy—Proper Management.	XVII. Disorders of Infancy.
VII. Miscarriage—Cause and Prevention.	XVIII. Disorders of Childhood.
	XIX. Training of Children.
VIII. Presentations and Positions.	XX. Hygiene of Infancy.
IX. The Fœtus in Utero.	XXI. Raising Children by Hand.
X. Parturition—Preparation.	XXII. Accidents and Emergencies.
XI. Diseases during Pregnancy.	XXIII. Poisons and Antidotes.

Every prospective mother ought to peruse this work, and learn how to properly prepare herself for the event. It will teach her exactly what she needs to know, and what may be learned no where else. It will prove a most useful charity— yea, an inestimable blessing—to the considerate man who bestows the book on the one who is to bring joy and gladness— through anxious periods — to his household. Will he not grant her this trifling boon ?

The above gives a fair idea of the nature and scope of this work. It will be seen that it covers the whole ground, and, if it is carefully read, will go far towards giving us an "ENLIGHTENED AND A HEALTHFUL MOTHERHOOD."

Ladies wanted to act as Agents for this work. Send stamp for terms. Copies sent by mail, post-paid, on receipt of price, plain, $1. Fine $1.25. Address S. R. WELLS, 389 Broadway, N.Y.

Works of a Kindred Nature.
SUPPLIED BY S. R. WELLS, 389 BROADWAY, N. Y.

Infancy. Physiological and Moral Management. Dr. Combe, $1.50.—Hereditary Descent, its Laws and Facts. $1.50.—Children: Their Diseases and Management. $1.75.—Philosophy of Generation, Abuses, etc. 50 cts.—Pregnancy and Childbirth. 50 cts. Chastity: Lectures for the Young. 50 cts.—Home Treatment, for Sexual Abuses. 50 cts.—Amativeness : Perverted Sexuality. 25 cts.—Uterine Diseases; or, Displacements of the Uterus. Illustrated. $5. —Sexual Diseases, Causes, Prevention and Cure. $2.00.—Midwifery and Diseases of Women. $1.75.—Animal Fertility: The Population Question. 25 cents.—Maternity: Bearing and Nursing of Children. $1.50.—Chronic Diseases; or, Nervous Diseases of Women. 50 cents.—Parent's Guide, Human Development, through Pre-Natal Influences. $1.50. See " Special List."

BOGLE & LYLES,
Grocers' Sundries.

PROPRIETORS OF THE

Renowned "A" Brand, Hermetically Sealed

FRUITS, VEGETABLES,
ETC., ETC.

Sole Proprietors of the celebrated "B and L" Brand of

IRISH OAT-MEAL.

AGENTS FOR

RICHARDSON & ROBBINS'

CHOICE

Canned Fruits, Dessert Fruits, Potted Meats,
ETC., ETC.

87 & 89 PARK PLACE, NEW YORK.

These goods are fast gaining the reputation their SUPERIOR QUALITY demands, and notwithstanding the great competition in this trade, now stand at the HEAD OF THE LIST. A trial of them will prove that they are the best in the market.

"GOOD BOOKS FOR ALL."
Published by S. R. WELLS, 389 Broadway, N. Y.

Best Works on these subjects. Each covers ground not covered by others. Copies sent by return post, on receipt of price. Please address us above.

American Phrenological Journal and Life Illustrated. Devoted to Ethnology, Physiology, Phrenology, Physiognomy, Psychology, Biography, Education, Art, Literature, with Measures to Reform, Elevate and Improve Mankind Physically, Mentally and Spiritually. Monthly, $3 a year.

Annuals of Phrenology and Physiognomy. One yearly 12mo volume. Price 25 cents for the current year. For 1865, '66, 67, '68, '69, 70, '71, '72 and '73. The nine containing over 400 pages, many portraits, with articles on "How to Study Phrenology," "Bashfulness, Diffidence, Stammering," "Marriage of Cousins," "Jealousy, Its Cause and Cure," etc. Bound in one vol., $2.

Constitution of Man. Considered in relation to External Objects. By George Combe. The only authorized American Edition. Twenty Engravings, and a Portrait of Author. $1.75.

Chart for Recording Development, 10 cents.

Chart of Physiognomy Illustrated for Framing. Map. 25 cents.

Defence of Phrenology. A Vindication of Phrenology against Attacks. The Cerebellum the seat of the reproductive instinct. Boardman. $1.50.

Domestic Life. Marriage Vindicated. Free Love Exposed. By Sizer. 25 cents.

Education. Founded on the Nature of Man. By J. G. Spurzheim. Appendix, with the Temperaments. $1.50.

Education and Self-Improvement Complete. Physiology—Animal and Mental; Self-Culture and Perfection of Character; Memory and Intellectual Improvement. In one vol. Muslin, $4.

Expression: Its Anatomy and Philosophy. By Sir Charles Bell. Illustrations. Notes by Editor *Phrenological Journal*. Fancy cloth. Fine. 1.50.

How to Read Character. A New Hand-Book of Phrenology and Physiognomy, for Students and Examiners, with a Chart for recording the sizes of the different Organs of the Brain, in the Delineation of Character. 170 Engravings. Latest and best. Paper, $1. Muslin, $1.25.

Memory and Intellectual Improvement, applied to Cultivation of Memory. Very useful. $1.50.

Lectures on Phrenology. By George Combe. The Phrenological Mode of Investigation. 1 vol. 12mo. $1.75.

Mental Science. The Philosophy of Phrenology. By Weaver. $1.50.

Moral Philosophy. By George Combe. Or, the Duties of Man considered in his Individual, Domestic and Social Capacities. Latest Ed. $1.75.

Natural Laws of Man. Questions with Answers. A Capital Work. By J. G. Spurzheim, M.D. Muslin, 75 cents.

New Physiognomy; or, Signs of Character, as manifested through Temperament and External Forms, and especially in the "Human Face Divine." With 1000 *Illustrations*. In three styles of binding. In muslin, $5; in heavy calf, $8; turkey morocco, full gilt, $10.

Phrenology and the Scriptures. Harmony between Phrenology and Bible. By Rev. John Pierpont. 25 cents.

Phrenological Bust. Showing the latest classification, and exact locations of the Organs of the Brain, for Learners. In this Bust, all the newly-discovered Organs are given. It is divided so as to show each Organ on one side; and all the groups—Social, Executive, Intellectual, and Moral—properly classified, on the other side. Two sizes; largest in box, $2.00; smaller, $1.00. Sent by express.

Phrenological Guide for Students, 25 cents.

Phrenology Proved, Illustrated and Applied. Analysis of the Primary Mental Powers in their Various Degrees of Development, and Location of the Phrenological Organs. $1.75.

Self-Culture and Perfection of Character; Including the Training and Management of Children. $1.50.

Self-Instructor in Phrenology and Physiology. 100 Engravings, Chart for Phrenologists. Pap. 50 cts. mus. 75 cts.

Symbolical Head and Phrenological Map, for Framing. 25 cents.

Wells' New Descriptive Chart for the Use of Examiners, giving a Delineation of Character. Illus. 25 cents.

Your Character from Your Likeness. Inclose stamp for a copy of circular, "Mirror of the Mind."

To Physicians, Lecturers, and Examiners. We have a Cabinet of 40 Casts of Heads, selected from Our Museum, which are sold at $35. Also a set of Phrenological Drawings on canvas, size of life, 40 in number, price $40. A set of six Anatomical and Physiological plates, colored and mounted, $20. Another set of twenty, in sheets, plain, $35. Colored and mounted, $60. Skeletons, from $50 to $100. Manikins, $500 to $1000. Portraits in oil from $5 upwards. Woodcuts, $3.50 to $5. Symbolical Heads, Electrotypes, $3 to $5, and $7.50, each

All Works pertaining to the "SCIENCE OF MAN," including Phrenology, Physiognomy, Ethnology, Psychology, Physiology, Anatomy, Hygiene, Dietetics, etc., supplied. Enclose stamp for Wholesale Terms.

Works on Physiology and Hygiene.

[It has been said that, a man at Forty Years of Age, is either "a Physician or a Fool." That at this Age, he ought to know how to treat, and take care of himself. These Works are intended to give instruction on "How to Live," and How to avoid Diseases.]

The Science of Health. A new Independent Health Monthly, which teaches the Laws by which Health is preserved, Disease eradicated, and Life prolonged, on Hygienic Principles. Its agencies are: Food, Drink, Air, Exercise, Light, Temperature, Sleep, Rest, Bathing, Clothing, Electricity, Right Social Relations, Mental Influences. It is a first-class Magazine, published at $2 a year.

Anatomical and Physiological PLATES Arranged expressly for Lectures on Health, Physiology, etc. By R. T. Trall, M.D. They are six in number, representing the normal position and life-size of all the internal viscera, magnified illustrations of the organs of the special senses, and a view of the nerves, arteries, veins, muscles, etc. Fully colored, backed, and mounted on rollers. Price for the set, net $20.

Avoidable Causes of Disease, INSANITY AND DEFORMITY. Marriage and its Violations. By Dr. Ellis. $2.

Accidents and Emergencies, What to Do—How to Do it. 25 cents.

Cure of Consumption by Mechanical Movements. By Dr. Wark, 30c.

Children, their Management in Health and Disease. By Dr. Shew. $1.75.

Diseases of the Throat and LUNGS. With Treatment. 25 cents.

Digestion and Dyspepsia. Complete Explanation of the Physiology of the Digestive Processes, Symptoms and Treatment of Dyspepsia and other Disorders of the Digestive Organs. Illus. By Dr. TRALL. New, Muslin, $1.

Philosophy of Electrical Psychology, in 12 Lectures. Dodds. $1.50.

Family Gymnasium. Gymnastic, Calisthenic, Kinesipathic, and Vocal Exercises, Development of the Bodily Organs. By Dr. Trall. Illus. $1.75.

Domestic Practice of Hydropathy. By E. Johnson, M.D. $2.

Hydropathic Cook Book. Recipes for Cooking on Hygienic Principles, $1.50.

Food and Diet. With Dietetical Regimen suited for Disordered States of the Digestive Organs. Dietaries of Principal Metropolitan Establishments for Lunatics, Criminals, Children, the Sick, Paupers, etc. A Scientific Work. By Pereira. Edited by Dr. C. A. Lee. $1.75.

Fruits and Farinacea, the PROPER FOOD OF MAN. By Dr. Smith. With Notes by Dr. Trall. $1.75.

Hydropathic Encyclopedia. A System of Hydropathy and Hygiene. Outlines of Anatomy; Physiology of the Human Body; Hygienic Agencies, Preservation of Health; Theory and Practice; Special Pathology, Nature, Causes, Symptoms, and Treatment of all known Diseases. A Guide to Families and Students, and a Text-Book for Physicians. By R. T. Trall, M.D. $4.50. "The most complete work on this subject." *Tribune.*

Hygienic Hand-Book. A Practical Guide for the Sick-Room. Alphabetically arranged. Appendix. Trall. $2.

Family Physician. A Ready Prescriber and Hygienic Adviser. With Reference to the Nature, Causes, Prevention and Treatment of Diseases, Accidents, and Casualties of every kind. With a Glossary and Copious Index. Illustrated. By Joel Shew, M.D. Muslin, $4.

Management of Infancy, Physiological and Moral Treatment. By Andrew Combe, M.D. Muslin, $1.50.

Medical Electricity. Manual for Students, Showing the scientific application to all forms of Acute and Chronic Diseases of the Different combinations of Electricity, Galvanism, Electro-Magnetism, Magneto-Electricity, and Human Magnetism. By Dr. White, $2.

Midwifery and the Diseases of Women. A Descriptive and Practical Work With the general management of Child-Birth, Nursery, etc. $1.75.

Movement-Cure (Swedish). History and Philosophy of this System of Medical Treatment, with Examples and Directions for their Use in Diseases. *Illustrated.* By Dr. Taylor. $1.75.

Notes on Beauty, Vigor and Development; or, How to Acquire Plumpness of Form, Strength of Limb, and Beauty of Complexion. 12 cents.

Paralysis and other Affections of the Nerves; Cure by Vibratory and Special Movements. Dr. Taylor. $1.

Physiology of Digestion. Considered with relation to the Principles of Dietetics. *Illus.* Combe. 50 cents.

Parents' Guide; or, Human Development through Inherited Tendencies. By Mrs. Hester Pendleton, Second ed., revised and enlarged. 1 vol. 18mo, $1.50.

Philosophy of Mesmerism and Clairvoyance. Six Lectures, with Introduction, 50 cents.

Philosophy of Sacred History, considered in Relation to Human Aliment and the Wines of Scripture. By Sylvester Graham, $3.00.

Philosophy of Water Cure. Development of the true Principles of Health and Longevity. Balbirnie. 50 cents.

Practice of Water Cure. Containing a Detailed account of the various Bathing processes. *Illus.* 50 cents.

Physiology, Animal and Mental: Applied to the Preservation and Restoration of Health, of Body and Power of Mind. *Illus.* Muslin, $1.50.

Principles of Physiology applied to the Preservation of Health and to the Improvement of Physical and Mental Education. By Andrew Combe. $1.75.

Sober and Temperate Life. Discourses and Letters of Cornaro. 50 cts.

Science of Human Life, Lectures on. By Sylvester Graham. With a copious Index and Biographical Sketch of the Author. *Illustrated.* $3.50.

Story of a Stomach. An Egotism. By a Reformed Dyspeptic. Mus. 75 cts.

Tea and Coffee, their Physical, Intellectual, and Moral Effects on the System. By Dr. Alcott. 25 cents.

Teeth; their Structure, Disease and Management, 25 cents.

Tobacco; Its Physical, Intellectual and Moral Effects, 25 cents.

The Alcoholic Controversy A Review of the *Westminster Review* on Errors of Teetotalism. Trall. 50 cents.

The Bath. Its History and Uses in Health and Disease. By R. T. Trall, M.D. Paper, 25 c.; muslin, 50 cents.

Three Hours' School a Day. A Serious Talk with Parents. $1.50.

The Human Feet. Their Shape, Dress and Proper Care, $1.25.

True Healing Art; or, Hygienic vs. Drug Medication. A practical view of the whole question. Pap. 30 c., mus. 50 c.

Water-Cure for the Million. The Processes Explained. Popular Errors Exposed. Hygienic and Drug Medication Contrasted, Rules for Bathing, Dieting, Exercising, etc. Pap., 30 cts., mus. 50 cts.

Water-Cure in Chronic Diseases. Causes, Progress, and Terminations of Various Diseases of the Digestive Organs, Lungs, Nerves and Skin, and their Treatment. By Dr. Gully. $2.

"**Special List**" of 70 or more Private Medical, Surgical and Anatomical Works, invaluable to those who need them, sent on receipt of stamp, by S. R. Wells, N.Y.

Works for Home Improvement.

This List embraces just such Works as are suited to every member of the family—useful to all, indispensable to those who have not the advantages of a liberal education.

Aims and Aids for Girls and Young Women, on the Duties of Life, Self-Culture, Dress, Beauty, Employment, Duties to Young Men, Marriage, and Happiness. By Weaver. $1.50.

Æsop's Fables. The People's Pictorial Edition. Beautifully Illustrated with nearly Sixty Engravings. Gilt. $1.

Carriage Painter's Illustrated Manual. Art, Science and Mystery of Coach, Carriage, and Car Painting. Fine Gilding, Bronzing, Staining, Varnishing, Polishing, Copying, Lettering, Scrolling, and Ornamenting. By Gardner. $1.00

Chemistry. Application to Physiology, Agriculture, Commerce. Liebig. 50 cents.

Conversion of St. Paul. By Geo. Jarvis Geer, D.D. 12mo. $1.

Footprints of Life; or, Faith and Nature Reconciled. A Poem in Three Parts. The Body, The Soul, The Deity. By Philip Harvey, M.D. $1.25.

Fruit Culture for the Million: A Hand-Book. Being a Guide to the Cultivation and Management of Fruit Trees. How to Propagate them. *Illus.* $1.

Gems of Goldsmith.—The Traveler. The Deserted Village. The Hermit. With notes and a sketch of the Great Author. *Illustrations.* Gilt. $1.

Good Man's Legacy. Rev. Dr. Osgood. 25 cents. **Gospel Among the Animals.** Same. 25 cents.

Hand-Book for Home Improvement: Comprising "How to Write," "How to Talk," "How to Behave," and "How to do Business." One vol. $2.25.

How to Live; Saving and Wasting, or, Domestic Economy made plain. $1.50.

How to Paint. A Complete Compendium of the Art. Designed for the Use of Tradesmen, Mechanics, Merchants, Farmers, and a Guide to the Professional Painter. By Gardner. $1.

Home for All; The Concrete, or Gravel Wall. Octagon. New, Cheap, Superior Mode of Building. $1.50.

Hopes and Helps for the Young of Both Sexes. Formation of Character, Choice of Avocation, Health, Conversation, Cultivation, Social Affection, Courtship, Marriage. Weaver. $1.50.

Library of Mesmerism and Psychology. Philosophy of Mesmerism, Clairvoyance, and Mental Electricity; Fascination, or the Power of Charming; The Macrocosm, or the World of Sense; Electrical Psychology, Doctrine of Impressions; The Science of the Soul, Physiologically and Philosophically. $4.

Life at Home; or, The Family and its Members. A capital work. By William Aikman, D.D. $1.50; gilt, $2.

Life in the West; or, Stories of the Mississippi Valley. Where to buy Public Lands. By N. C. Meeker. $2.

Man and Woman considered in their Relation to each other and to the World, By H. C. Pedder. $1.00.

Man, in Genesis and in Geology; or, the Biblical Account of Man's Creation, tested by Scientific Theories of his Origin and Antiquity. By Joseph P. Thompson, D.D., LL.D. One vol. $1.

Pope's Essay on Man. With Notes. Beautifully Illustrated. Cloth, gilt, beveled boards. Best edition. $1.

A Self-Made Woman; or, Mary Idyl's Trials and Triumphs. Suggestive of a noble and happy life. By Emma M. Buckingham. $1.50.

Oratory—Sacred and Secular or, the Extemporaneous Speaker. Including Chairman's Guide. $1.50.

Temperance in Congress. Ten Minutes' Speeches—powerful—delivered in the House of Representatives. 25 cts.

The Christian Household. Embracing Husband, Wife, Father, Mother, Child, Brother, Sister. Weaver. $1.

The Emphatic Diaglott; or, the New Testament in Greek and English. Containing the Original Greek Text of the New Testament, with an Interlineary Word-for-Word English Translation. By Wilson. Price $4, extra fine binding, $5.

Right Word in the Right Place. A New Pocket Dictionary Synonyms, Technical Terms, Abbreviations, Foreign Phrases, Writing for the Press Punctuation, Proof-Reading. 75 cents.

The Temperance Reformation. History from the first Temp. Society in U. S. By Armstrong. $1.50.

The Model Potato. The result of 20 years' investigation and experiment in cultivation and cooking. By McLarin Notes by R. T. Trall, M.D. 50 cents.

Thoughts for the Young Men and Young Women of America. By L. U. Reavis. Notes by Greeley. $1.00.

Ways of Life, Showing the Right Way and the Wrong Way. Weaver. $1.

Weaver's Works. "Hopes and Helps," "Aims and Aids," "Ways of Life." A great work, in one vol. $3.00.

Wedlock. Right Relations of the Sexes. Laws of Conjugal Selection. Who may and who may not Marry. For both Sexes. By Wells. Plain, $1.50; gilt, 2$.

Capital Punishment; or, the Proper Treatment of Criminals. 10 cents.

Education of the Heart. Colfax. 10 cents. **Father Matthew,** Temperance Apostle, Portrait, Character and Biography. 10 cents.

History of Salem Witchcraft; The Planchette Mystery; Modern Spiritualism, By Mrs. Stowe; and Dr. Doddridge's Celebrated Dream. 1 vol. $1.

Agents Wanted. There are many individuals in every neighborhood who would be glad to have one or more of these useful Books. Hundreds of Copies could be sold *where they have never yet been introduced.* A *Local Agent* is wanted in every town, to whom liberal terms will be given. This is one way to do good and be paid for it. Send stamp for Illustrated Catalogue, with terms to Agents.

Address, **S. R. WELLS, 389 Broadway, New York.**

Water-Cure in Chronic Diseases: an Exposition of the Causes, Progress, and Terminations of various Chronic Diseases of the Digestive Organs, Lungs, Nerves, Limbs, and Skin, and of their Treatment by Water and other Hygienic means. Illustrated with an engraved View of the Nerves of the Lungs, Heart, Stomach, and Bowels. By J. M. Gully, M.D. 12mo, 405 pp. Muslin, $2.

Domestic Practice of Hydropathy; with Fifteen Engraved Illustrations of important subjects, from Drawings by Dr. Howard Johnson, with a form of a Report for the assistance of Patients in consulting their Physician by correspondence. By Edward Johnson, M.D. 12mo, 467 pp. Muslin, $2.

Children: their Hydropathic Management in Health and Disease. A Descriptive and Practical Work, designed as a Guide for Families and Physicians. Illustrated with numerous cases. By Joel Shew, M.D. 12mo, 430 pp. $1.75.

Midwifery and the Diseases of Women: a Descriptive and Practical Work. With the General Management of Childbirth, Nursery, etc. Illustrated with numerous Cases of Treatment. Same author. 12mo, 430 pp. Muslin, $1.75.

Hydropathic Cook-Book; with Recipes for Cooking on Hygienic Principles. Containing also, a Philosophical Exposition of the Relations of Food to Health, the Chemical Elements and Proximate Constitution of Alimentary Principles, the Nutritive Properties of all kinds of Aliments, the Relative Value of Vegetable and Animal Substances, the Selection and Preservation of Dietetic Material, etc. By R. T. Trall, M.D. 12mo, 226 pp. Muslin, $1.50.

Philosophy of the Water-Cure: a Development of the True Principles of Health and Longevity. By John Balbirnie, M.D. Illustrated; with the Confessions and Observations of Sir Edward Lytton Bulwer. 12mo. 50 cents.

Practice of the Water-Cure; with Authenticated Evidence of its Efficacy and Safety. Containing a Detailed Account of the various processes used in the Water Treatment, a Sketch of the History and Progress of the Water-Cure, well authenticated cases of Cure, etc. By James Wilson and James Manby Gully, M.D. 12mo, 144 pp. Paper, 50 cents.

Diseases of the Throat and Lungs, including Diphtheria and their Proper Treatment. By R. T. Trall, M.D. With illustrative engravings. 12mo, pp. 39. Paper, 25 cents.

Water-Cure for the Million. The Processes of Water-Cure Explained in a practical and popular manner. 30 cents.

The True Healing Art; or, Hygienic vs. Drug Medication. 30 cts.

Sent prepaid by first post, at prices annexed. Local agents wanted.

Address **S. R. WELLS, 389 Broadway, New York.**

THE INDISPENSABLE HAND-BOOK.

How to Write---How to Talk----How to Behave, and How to Do Business.

COMPLETE IN ONE LARGE VOLUME.

THIS new work—in four parts—embraces just that practical matter-of-fact information which every one—old and young—ought to have. It will aid in attaining, if it does not insure, "success in life." It contains some 600 pages, elegantly bound, and is divided into four parts, as follows:

How to Write:

AS A MANUAL OF LETTER-WRITING AND COMPOSITION, IS FAR SUPERIOR to the common "Letter-Writers." It teaches the inexperienced how to write Business Letters, Family Letters, Friendly Letters, Love Letters, Notes and Cards, and Newspaper Articles, and how to Correct Proof for the Press. The rewspapers have pronounced it "Indispensable."

How to Talk:

NO OTHER BOOK CONTAINS SO MUCH USEFUL INSTRUCTION ON THE subject as this. It teaches how to Speak Correctly, Clearly, Fluently, Forcibly, Eloquently, and Effectively, in the Shop, in the Drawing-room; a Chairman's Guide, to conduct Debating Societies and Public Meetings; how to Spell, and how to Pronounce all sorts of Words; with Exercises for Declamation. The chapter on "Errors Corrected" is worth the price of the volume to every young man. "Worth a dozen grammars."

How to Behave:

THIS IS A MANUAL OF ETIQUETTE, AND IT IS BELIEVED TO BE THE best "MANNERS BOOK" ever written. If you desire to know what good manners require, at Home, on the Street, at a Party, at Church, at Table, in Conversation, at Places of Amusement, in Traveling, in the Company of Ladies, in Courtship, this book will inform you. It is a standard work on Good Behavior.

How to Do Business:

INDISPENSABLE IN THE COUNTING-ROOM, IN THE STORE, IN THE SHOP, on the FARM, for the Clerk, the Apprentice, the Book Agent, and for Business Men. It teaches how to Choose a Pursuit, and how to follow it with success. "It teaches how to get rich honestly," and how to use your riches wisely.

How to Write—How to Talk—How to Behave—How to Do Business, bound in one large handsome volume, post-paid, for $2 25.

Agents wanted. Address, S. R. WELLS, 389 Broadway, New York.

FOOD FOR DYSPEPTICS.
Dr. TRALLS
GRAHAM CRACKERS.

These will be found a most wholesome and nutritious article of food for DYSPEPTICS and INVALIDS, whose Digestive Organs are so weak, that the other preparations of Wheat and other foods are not easily digested. These Crackers will be found exceedingly palatable and very nutritious. Put up in packages of

10 lbs. $1.40.   15 lbs. $2.10.   20 lbs. $2.75.

Barrels and Half Barrels at reduced rates.

Something New.
OAT MEAL CRACKERS,
WHOLESOME AND PALATABLE. TRY THEM.

All kinds of Crackers and Biscuits supplied at lowest prices.

J. A. CURRIER, Sole Proprietor,

436 Greenwich Street, N. Y.

ASK YOUR GROCER FOR THEM.

WORKS ON
HYDROPATHY, OR WATER-CURE.
PUBLISHED BY
S. R. WELLS, 389 Broadway, N. Y.

Hydropathic Encyclopedia: a System of Hydropathy and Hygiene. In 1 large octavo volume. Embracing Outlines of Anatomy—illustrated; Physiology of the Human Body; Hygienic Agencies, and the Preservation of Health; Dietetics and Hydropathic Cookery; Theory and Practice of Water-Treatment; Special Pathology and Hydro-Therapeutics, including the Nature, Causes, Symptoms, and Treatment of all Known Diseases; Application of Hydropathy to Midwifery and the Nursery; with nearly 1000 pages, including a Glossary, Table of Contents, and a complete Index. Designed as a Guide to Families and Students, and a Text-Book for Physicians. With 300 engraved illustrations. By R. T. Trall, M.D. $4.50.

In the general plan and arrangement of the work, the wants and necessities of the people have been steadily kept in view. Whilst almost every topic of interest in the departments of Anatomy, Physiology, Pathology, Hygiene, and Therapeutics is briefly presented, those of practical utility are always put prominently forward. The prevailing conceits and whims of the day and age are exposed and refuted; the theories and hypotheses upon which the popular drug-practice is predicated are controverted, and the why and wherefore of their fallacy clearly demonstrated.

It is a rich, comprehensive, and well-arranged encyclopedia.—*New York Tribune.*

Anatomical and Physiological Plates. These Plates were arranged expressly for Lecturers on Health, Physiology, etc., by R. T. Trall, M.D., of the New York Hydropathic College. They are six in number, representing the normal position and life-size of all the internal viscera, magnified illustrations of the organs of the special senses, and a view of the principal nerves, arteries, veins, muscles, etc. For popular instruction, for families, schools, and for professional reference, they will be found far superior to any thing of the kind heretofore published, as they are more complete and perfect in artistic design and finish. Price for the set, fully colored, backed, and mounted on rollers, sent by express, not mailable, (net) $20.

The Hygienic Hand-Book: a Practical Guide for the Sick-Room, with Appendix. By R. T. Trall. One vol. 12mo, price $2.

A new and carefully-revised edition of this work has just been issued, which should be in the hands of all who would get well and keep well without drugs.

Hydropathic Family Physician: a Ready Prescriber and Hygienic Adviser. With Reference to the Nature, Causes, Prevention, and Treatment of Diseases, Accidents, and Casualties of every kind. With a Glossary and copious Index. By Joel Shew, M.D. Illustrated with nearly 300 engravings. One large volume, intended for use in the family. 12mo, 816 pp. Muslin, $4.

It possesses the most practical utility of any of the author's contributions to popular medicine, and is well adapted to give the reader an accurate idea of the organization and functions of the human frame.—*New York Tribune.*

www.ingramcontent.com/pod-product-compliance
Lightning Source LLC
Chambersburg PA
CBHW031606110426
42742CB00037B/1310